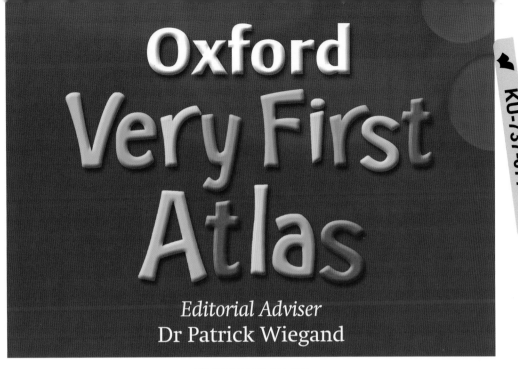

Oxford Very First Atlas

Editorial Adviser
Dr Patrick Wiegand

OXFORD
UNIVERSITY PRESS

Great Clarendon Street, Oxford OX2 6DP

Oxford University Press is a department of the University of Oxford.
It furthers the University's objective of excellence in research, scholarship,
and education by publishing worldwide in

Oxford   New York

Auckland Cape Town Dar es Salaam Hong Kong Karachi
Kuala Lumpur Madrid Melbourne Mexico City Nairobi
New Delhi Shanghai Taipei Toronto

With offices in

Argentina Austria Brazil Chile Czech Republic France Greece
Guatemala Hungary Italy Japan Poland Portugal Singapore
South Korea Switzerland Thailand Turkey Ukraine Vietnam

Oxford is a registered trade mark of Oxford University Press
in the UK and in certain other countries

© Oxford University Press 2009

First published 2009

© Maps copyright Oxford University Press

Cover illustrations by Bernice Lam

The moral rights of the authors have been asserted.

ISBN 978 0 19 838747 3 (hardback)
ISBN 978 0 19 838748 0 (paperback)

1 3 5 7 9 10 8 6 4 2

Printed in Singapore

Paper used in the production of this book is a natural, recyclable product
made from wood grown in sustainable forests. The manufacturing process
conforms to the environmental regulations of the country of origin.

Acknowledgements

The publishers would like to thank Roderick Hunt for his advice on literacy levels.

The publishers would like to thank the following for permission to reproduce photographs:

Alamy pp 13 (Roger Cracknell), 22 (Visions of America, LLC), 23 (Gary Cook), 25 (Dave Watts),
26 (PeterArnold Inc.), 27 (Steven J. Kazlowski), 29 (John Macpherson); Photolibrary Group pp7 (Radius Images),
21 (Jochen Tack), 32 (Brian Lawrence); Science Photo Library pp 5 (Planetary Visions Ltd), 6 (Planetary Visions
Ltd), 8t (Planetary Visions Ltd), 8b (Planetobserver), 10-11 (Planetobserver), 28 (Planetobserver).
All other photographs supplied by Oxford University Press.

Contents

Greetings from **THE ALPS**

Look at pages 18–19.

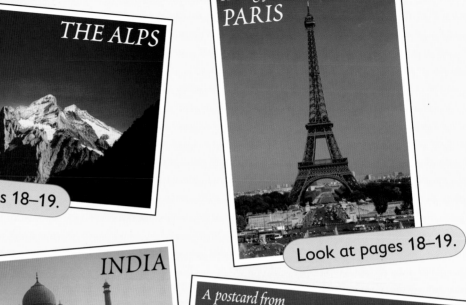

Having fun in **PARIS**

Look at pages 18–19.

On holiday in **INDIA**

Look at pages 20–21.

A postcard from **NEW YORK**

Look at page 22.

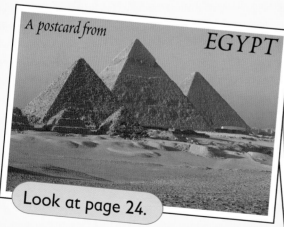

A postcard from **EGYPT**

Look at page 24.

Greetings from **LONDON**

Look at page 32.

2 Can you find these places in the atlas?

4 This is space.

The Earth is a planet in space.

6 The Earth is round, like a ball.

Satellites take pictures of the Earth.

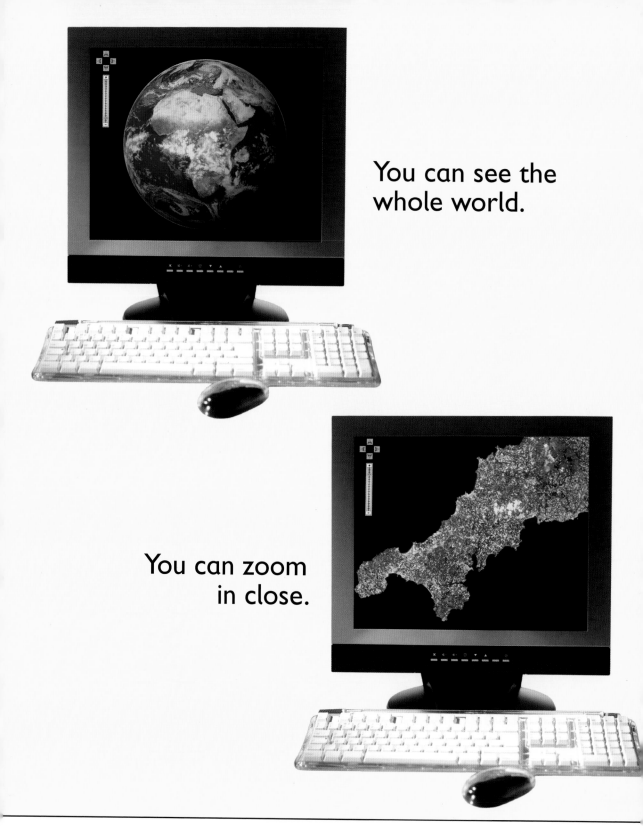

You can see the whole world.

You can zoom in close.

These are satellite pictures on a computer.

The Earth has land and sea.

A globe is a model of the Earth.

10 This is a picture of the Earth from space.

It is laid out flat.

The World

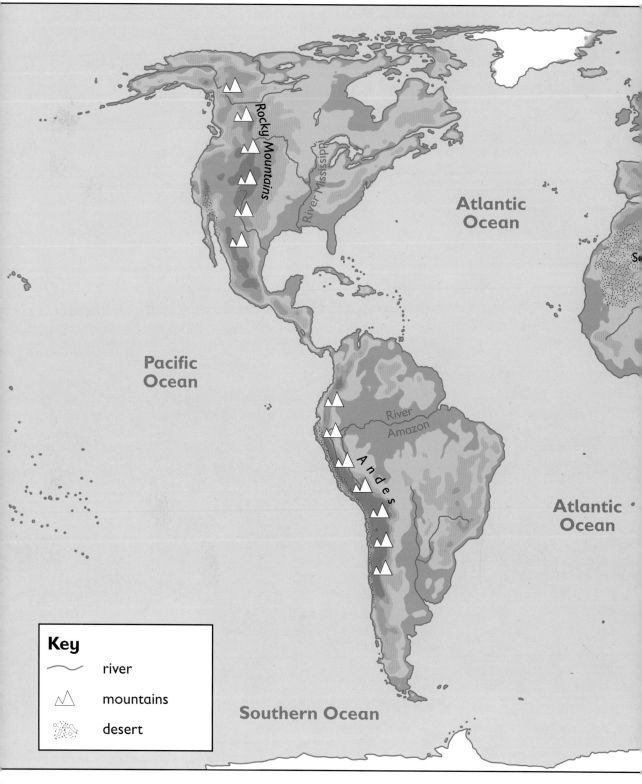

Rocky Mountains

River Mississippi

Atlantic Ocean

Pacific Ocean

River Amazon

Andes

Atlantic Ocean

Southern Ocean

Key
~ river
△ mountains
▵ desert

This is a map of the world.

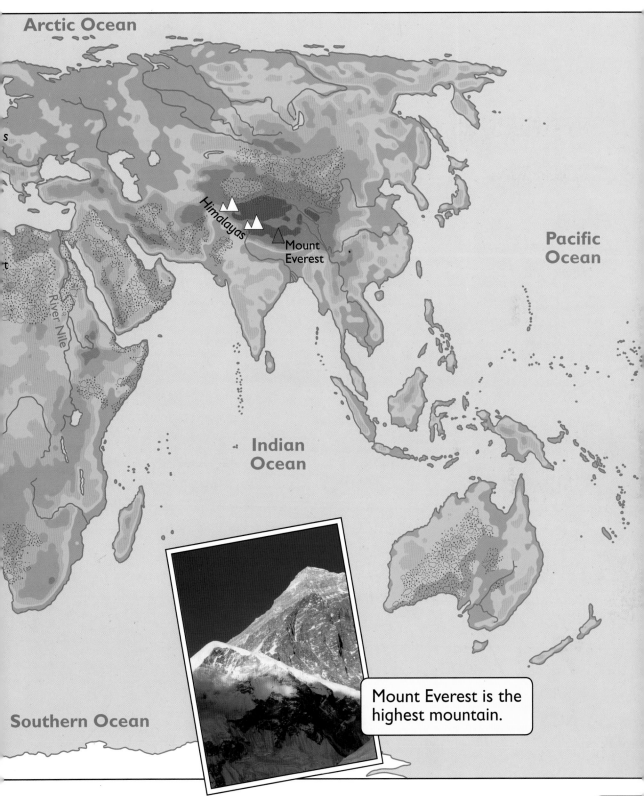

Arctic Ocean

Himalayas

Mount
Everest

Pacific
Ocean

River Nile

Indian
Ocean

Southern Ocean

Mount Everest is the
highest mountain.

It shows rivers, mountains and deserts.

The World

North America

South America

This is a map of Antarctica.

Antarctica

South Pole

The world has seven continents.

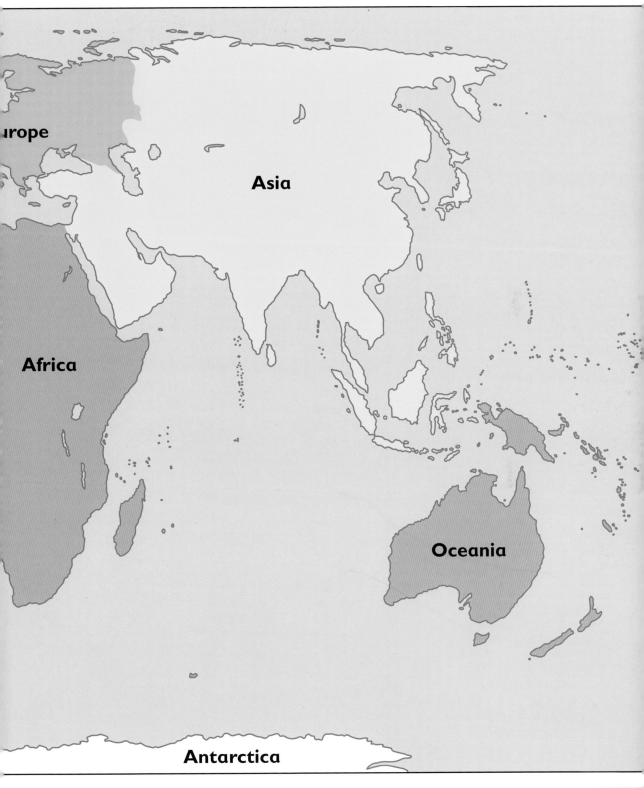

Europe

Asia

Africa

Oceania

Antarctica

Continents are very big areas of land.

The World

Canada

United Kingdom

United States
of America

Fr

Sp

Morocco

Mexico

M

Colombia

Brazil

Peru

Bolivia

Chile

Argentina

Key

Colours show
countries.

The world has many countries.

Russia

Japan

China

Iran

Pakistan

bya

Egypt

Saudi
Arabia

India

Philippines

Chad

Sudan

Ethiopia

Kenya

Tanzania

Indonesia

Angola

Madagascar

Australia

South
Africa

New
Zealand

Which country are you from?

Europe

Iceland
Reykjavik

Sweden

Norway
Oslo

Stockho

Denmark
Copenhage

United
Kingdom

Republic
of Ireland
Dublin

Berlin

Pol

London

Netherlands

Germany

Belgium

Prague Czec
Repub

Paris

River Danube

Vie

Switzerland

Austria

France

Alps

Italy
Rome

Portugal

Madrid

Lisbon

Spain

Mal

Key

Colours show
countries.

■ capital cities

~ river

△ mountains

Europe is a small continent.

Finland

Helsinki

Tallinn
Estonia

Riga
Latvia

thuania
Vilnius

Minsk

Belarus

saw

Kiev

Ukraine

Romania

grade
Bucharest

Bulgaria
Sofia

reece

Athens

Cyprus

Russia

River Volga

Moscow

Georgia
Tbilisi

Ankara

Turkey

Hello   Hola   Buon giorno

God dag   Guten Tag

Bonjour   Yia sas

Dzień dobry   Merhaba

There are many European languages.

19

Asia

Moscow

Russia

Astana ■

Kazakhstan

Ulan Bator ■

Mongolia

Uzbekistan Tashkent ■

Gobi Desert

Beijing ■

Turkmenistan
Ashgabat

China

Tehran ■

Afghanistan Kabul ■

Baghdad ■

Islamabad ■

Iraq Iran

Pakistan

Himalayas

Yangtze River

Riyadh ■

Muscat ■

New
Delhi ■

Bangladesh
Dhaka

Hanoi ■

Saudi
Arabia Oman

India

Myanmar

Yangon

Sana ■ Yemen

Bangkok Thailand

Manila ■

Vietnam

Philippines

Kuala Lumpur

Malaysia

Jakarta ■ Indones

20 Asia is the largest continent.

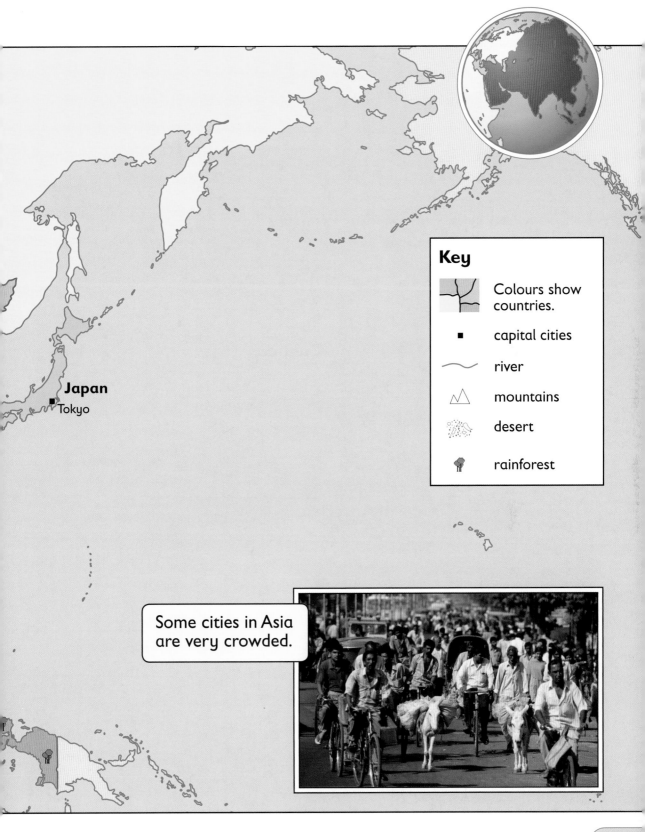

Key

Colours show countries.

■ capital cities

〜 river

⋀ mountains

desert

rainforest

Japan
Tokyo

Some cities in Asia are very crowded.

It also has the most people.

North America

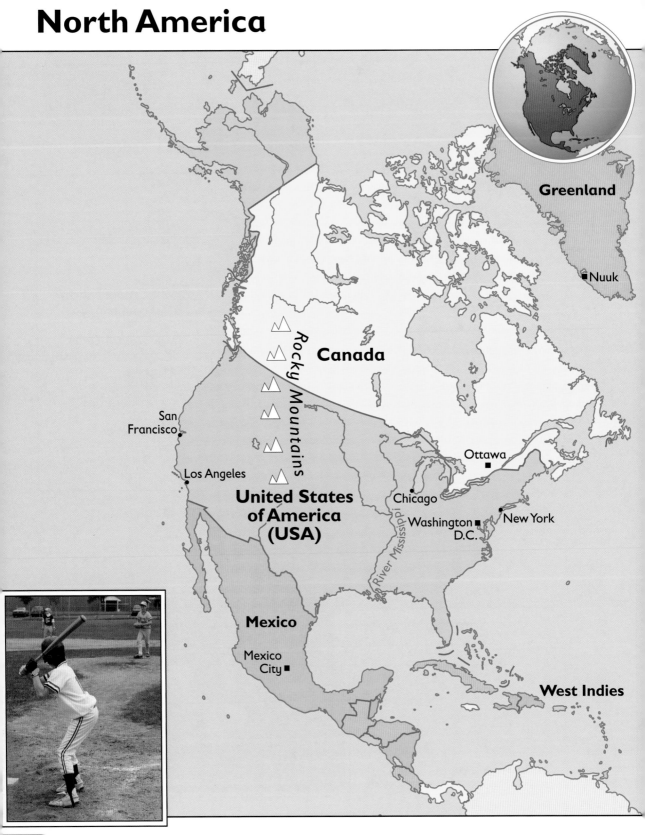

Greenland

Nuuk

Rocky Mountains

Canada

San Francisco

Los Angeles

United States of America (USA)

Ottawa

Chicago

Washington D.C.

New York

River Mississippi

Mexico

Mexico City

West Indies

The USA is the world's richest country.

South America

Caracas

Venezuela

Bogota

Colombia

Georgetown

Paramaribo
Cayenne

Suriname

French Guiana

Guyana

Quito
Ecuador

River Amazon

B r a z i l

Lima

Peru

Bolivia

La Paz

Brasilia

Paraguay

Asuncion

Argentina

Santiago

Uruguay

Buenos Aires

Montevideo

Key

Colours show
countries.

■ capital cities

• other cities

river

mountains

rainforest

It rains a lot in the
Amazon rainforest.

There is a big rainforest in Brazil.

Africa

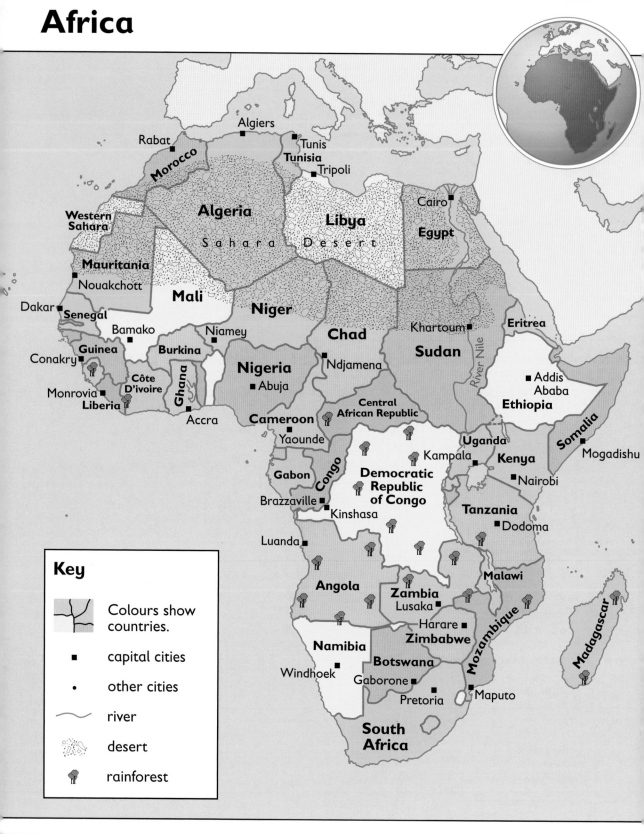

Key

Colours show countries.

■   capital cities

•   other cities

〜   river

desert

rainforest

Africa is the hottest continent.

Oceania

Nauru

Papua New Guinea

Port Moresby

Solomon Islands

Tuvalu

Vanuatu

Fiji

New Caledonia

Great Sandy Desert

A u s t r a l i a

Great Victoria Desert

Perth

Brisbane

Adelaide

Sydney

Canberra

Melbourne

New Zealand

Wellington

Australia has many strange animals.

There are lots of islands in Oceania.

Antarctica

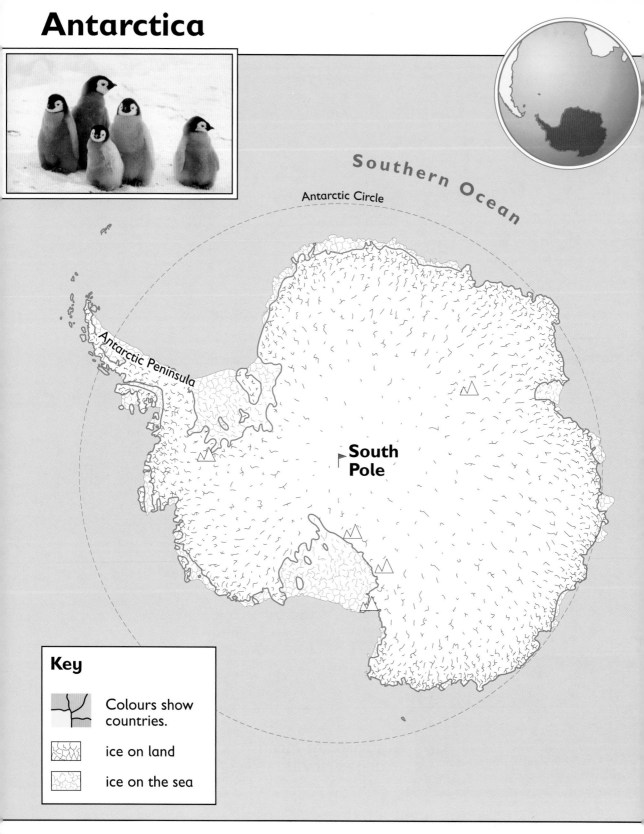

Southern Ocean

Antarctic Circle

Antarctic Peninsula

South Pole

Key

Colours show countries.

ice on land

ice on the sea

Antarctica is land covered in ice.

The Arctic Ocean

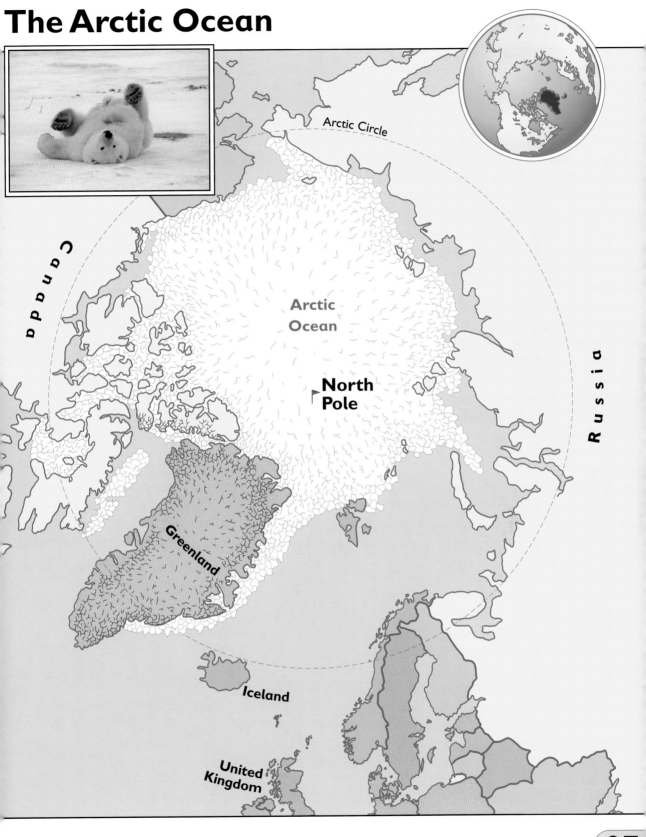

Arctic Circle

Canada

Arctic
Ocean

North
Pole

Russia

Greenland

Iceland

United
Kingdom

The Arctic Ocean is frozen water.

28 This is Great Britain and Ireland from space

The British Isles

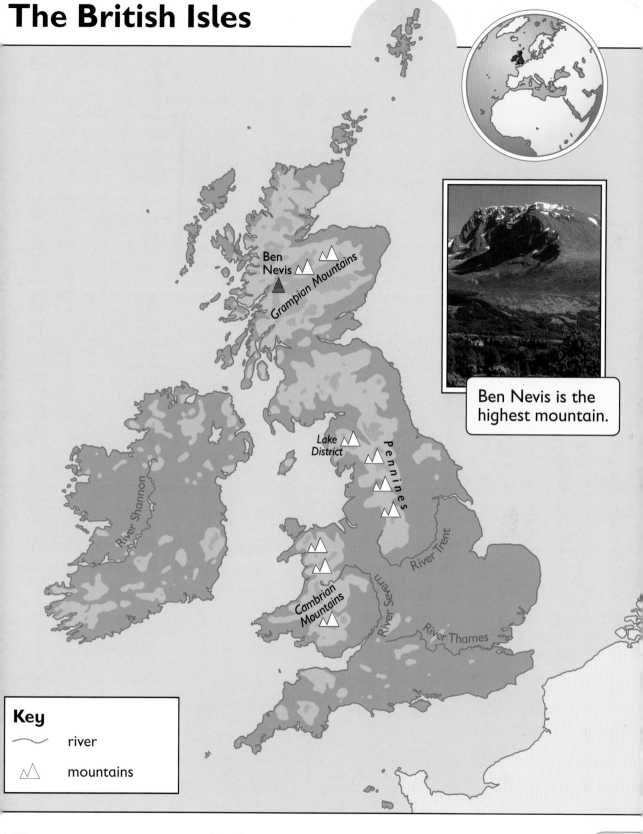

Ben
Nevis

Grampian Mountains

Lake
District

Pennines

River Shannon

River Trent

Cambrian
Mountains

Severn

River Thames

Ben Nevis is the
highest mountain.

Key

~~~ river

/\ mountains

This is a map of Great Britain and Ireland.

The British Isles

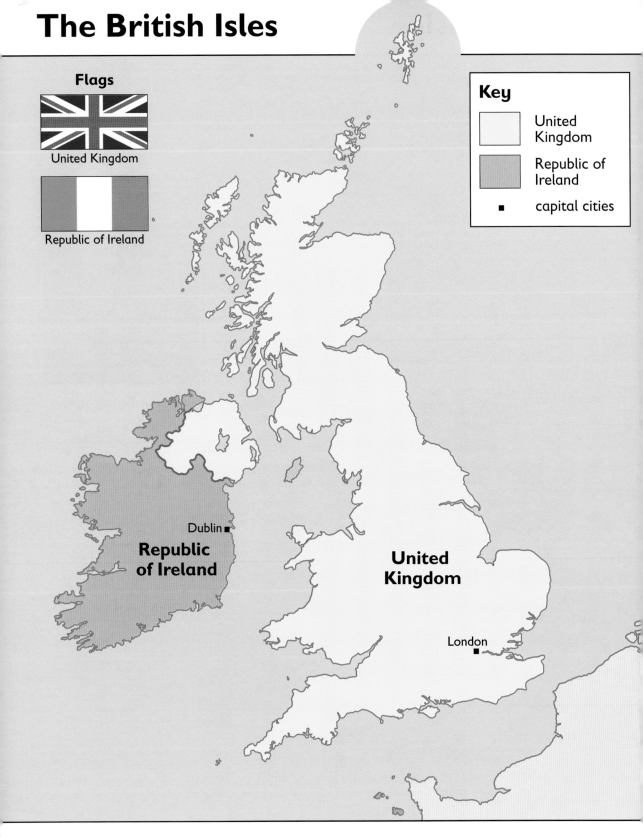

Flags

United Kingdom

Republic of Ireland

Key

United Kingdom

Republic of Ireland

■ capital cities

Dublin ■

Republic of Ireland

United Kingdom

London ■

There are two countries in the British Isles

The United Kingdom

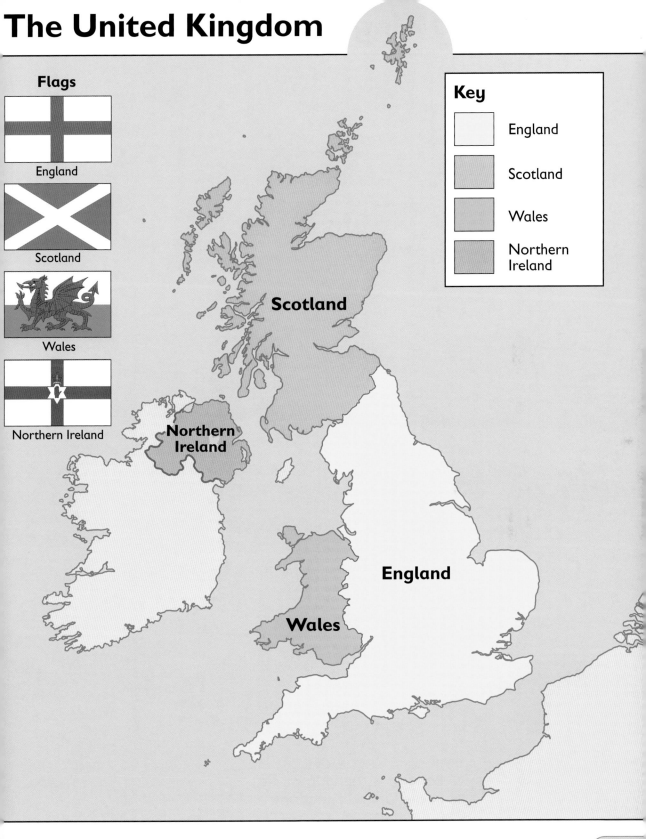

Flags

England

Scotland

Wales

Northern Ireland

Key

England

Scotland

Wales

Northern Ireland

Scotland

Northern Ireland

England

Wales

The United Kingdom has four parts.

The United Kingdom

Key
- ■ capital cities
- • other big cities

Scotland

Glasgow ■Edinburgh

Northern
Ireland ■
Belfast

•Newcastle upon Tyne

Leeds•
Liverpool Manchester•
•Sheffield
Nottingham•

England

Norwich•

•Birmingham

Wales

Cardiff
■ •Bristol

London ■

Southampton•

London is the biggest city
in the United Kingdom.

There are many big cities.